TODDLER
Christmas
Coloring Book

Holiday Coloring and Activity Book for Toddlers and Preschoolers

PRESCHOOL ACTIVITY WORKBOOKS

Copyright © 2017 DGT Book Promotions, LLC
Published by DGT Book Promotions, LLC
All rights reserved. Interior art obtained via 123rf.com and public domain from
pixabay.com under a Creative Commons Zero 1.0 License.
Cover art obtained through 123rf.com
ISBN-13: 978-1979639057   ISBN-10: 1979639051

THE *TODDLER CHRISTMAS COLORING BOOK* IS PERFECT FOR KEEPING YOUR TODDLER OR PRESCHOOL AGE CHILD ENTERTAINED AND BUSY THIS CHRISTMAS HOLIDAY SEASON WHILE ALSO HELPING THEM TO DEVELOP THE FINE MOTOR CONTROL THEY NEED FOR THE FUTURE AS THEY COLOR THESE FUN SIMPLE COLORING PAGES.

WHAT'S INSIDE:

- LARGE 8 X 10 INCH PAGES
- 30 FUN PICTURES TO COLOR
- 30 DUPLICATE COLORING PAGES YOU CAN COLOR WITH YOUR CHILD OR THEY CAN SHARE WITH A FRIEND

What do you want for Christmas?

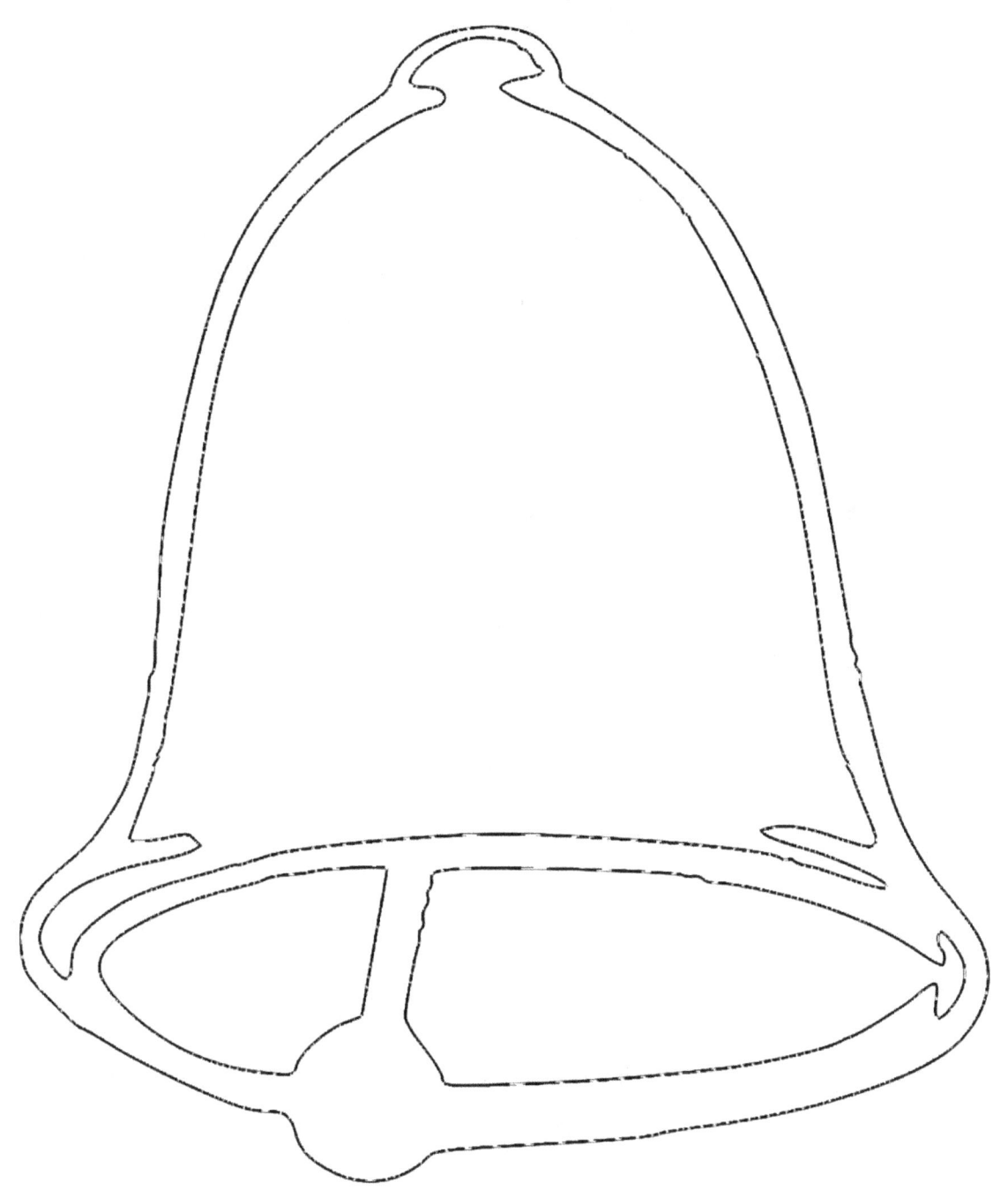

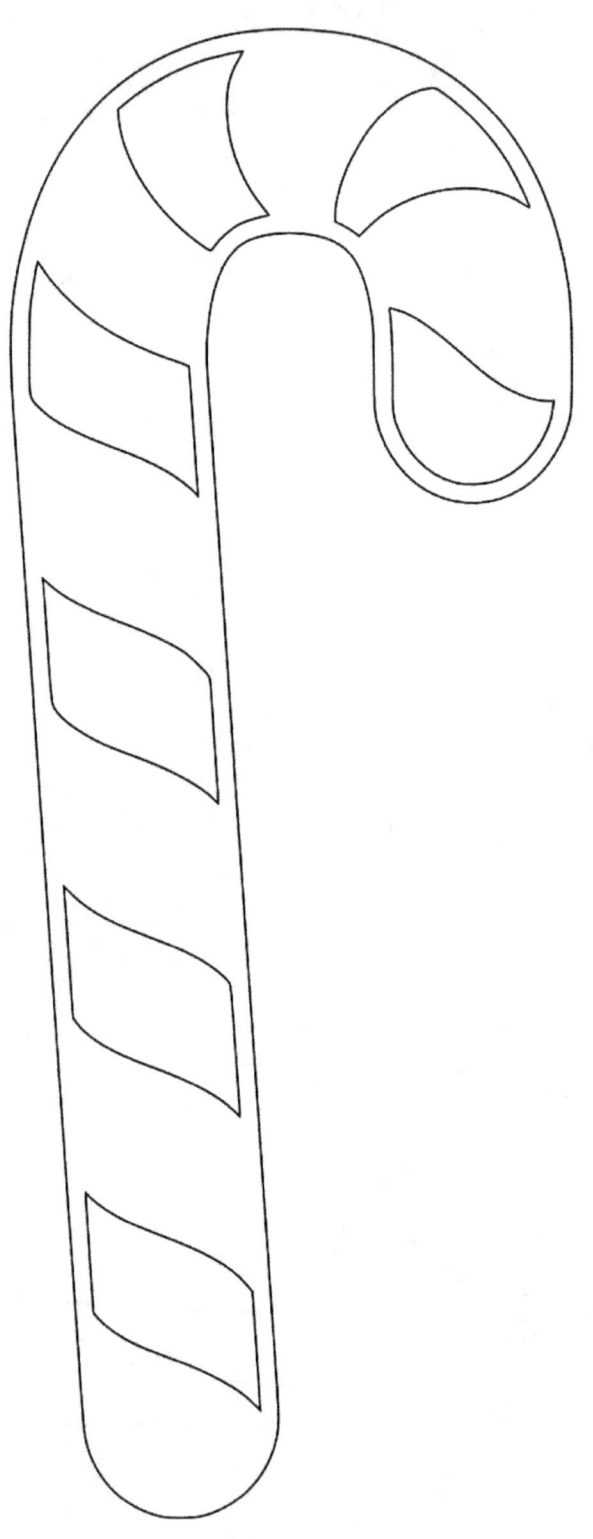

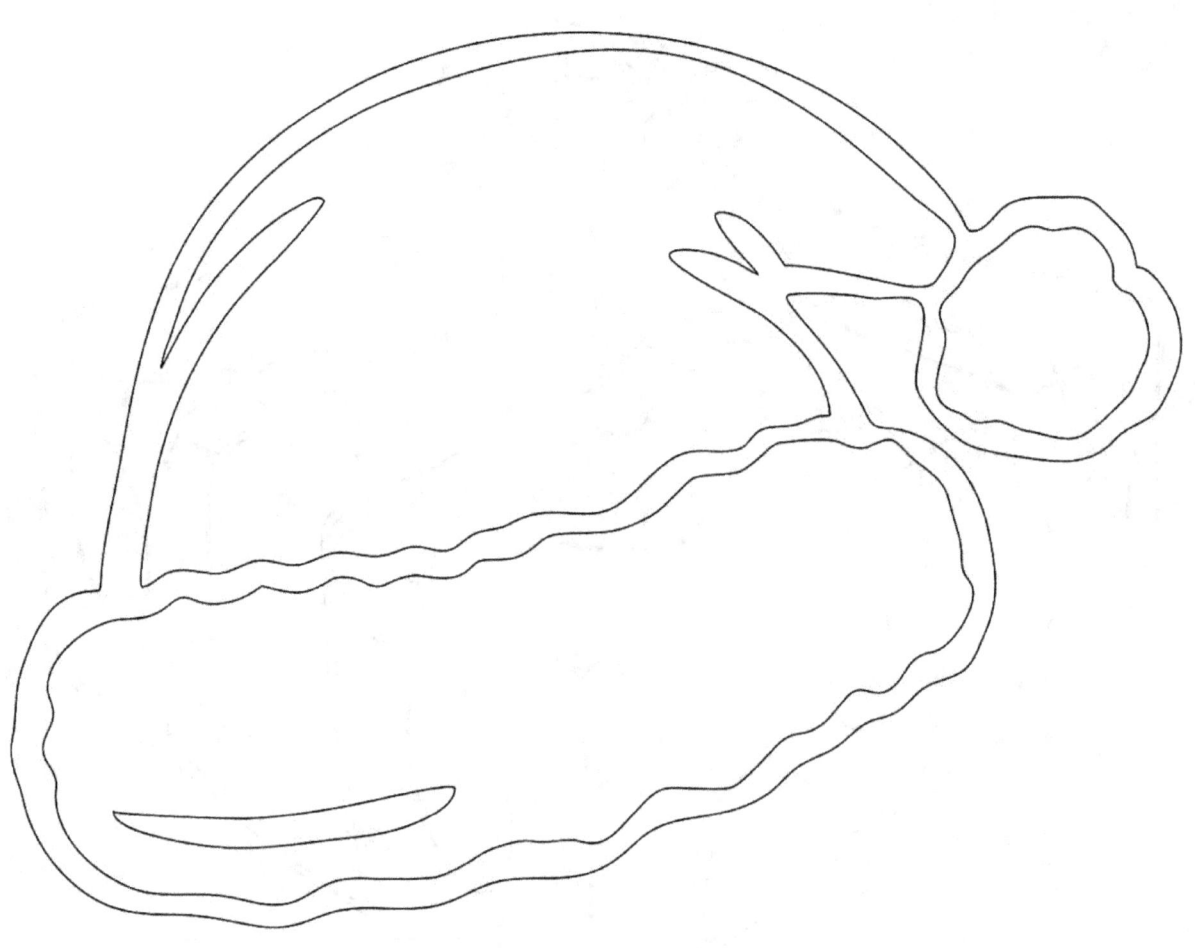

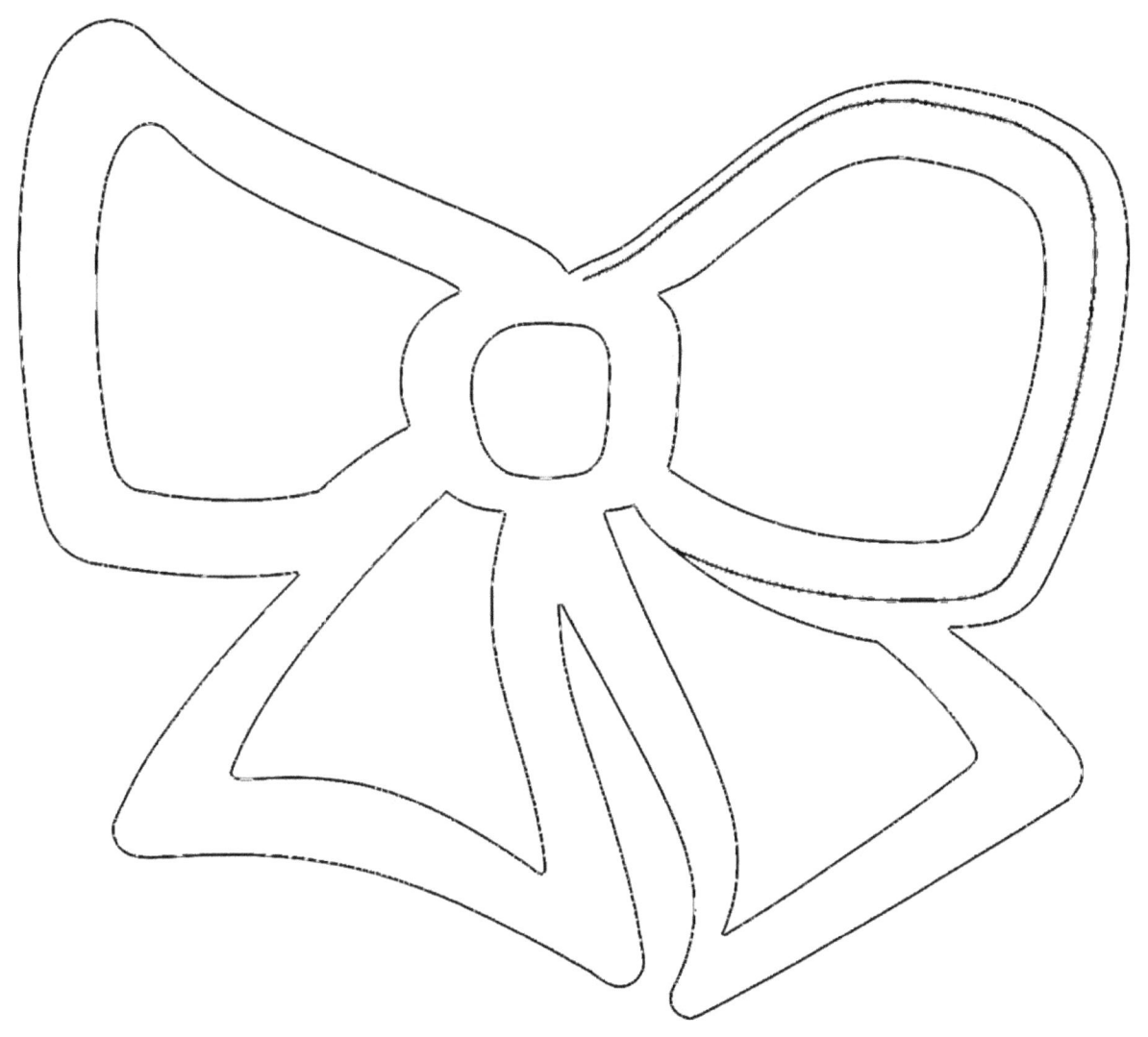

Share a coloring page with a friend

What do you want for Christmas?

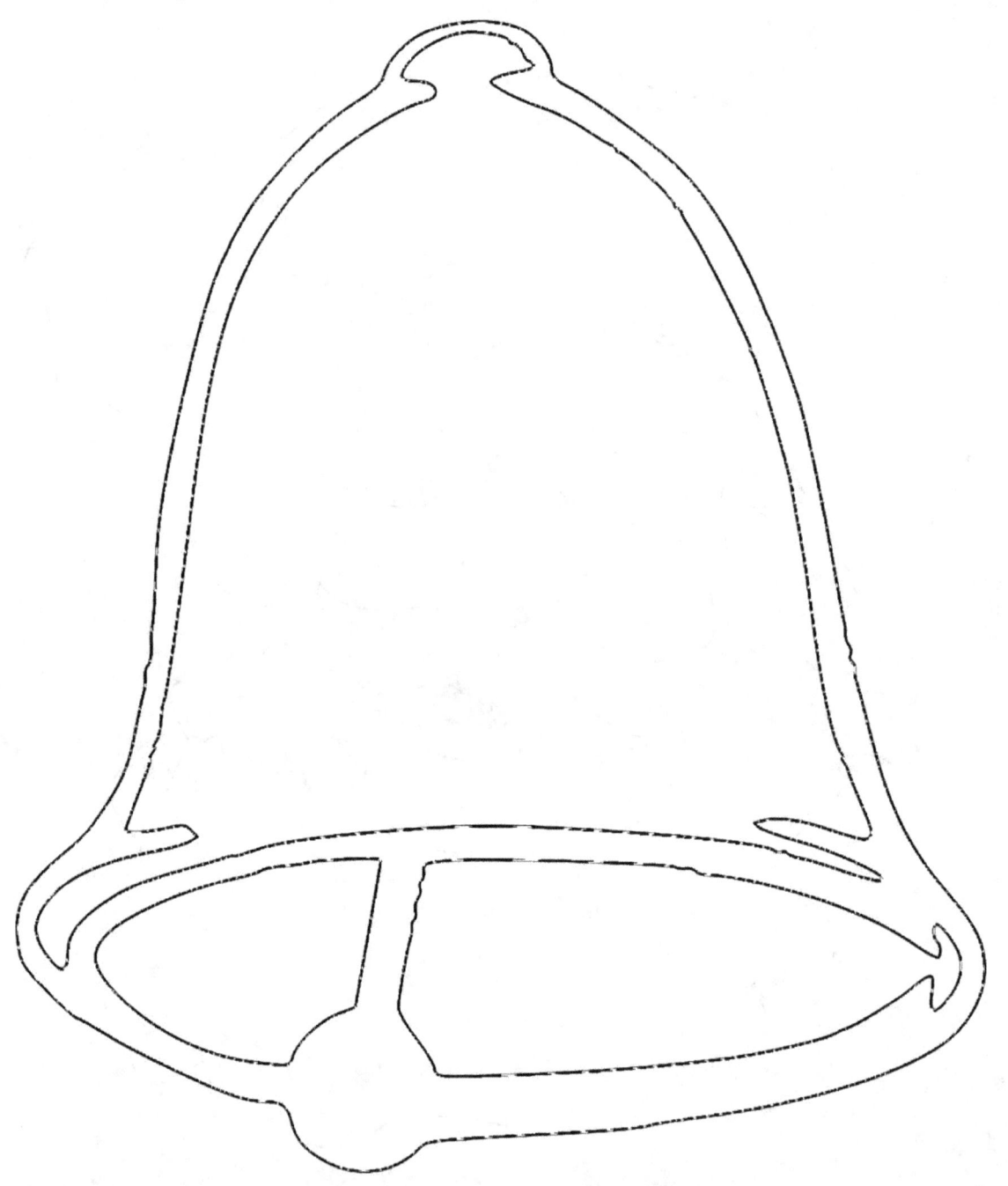

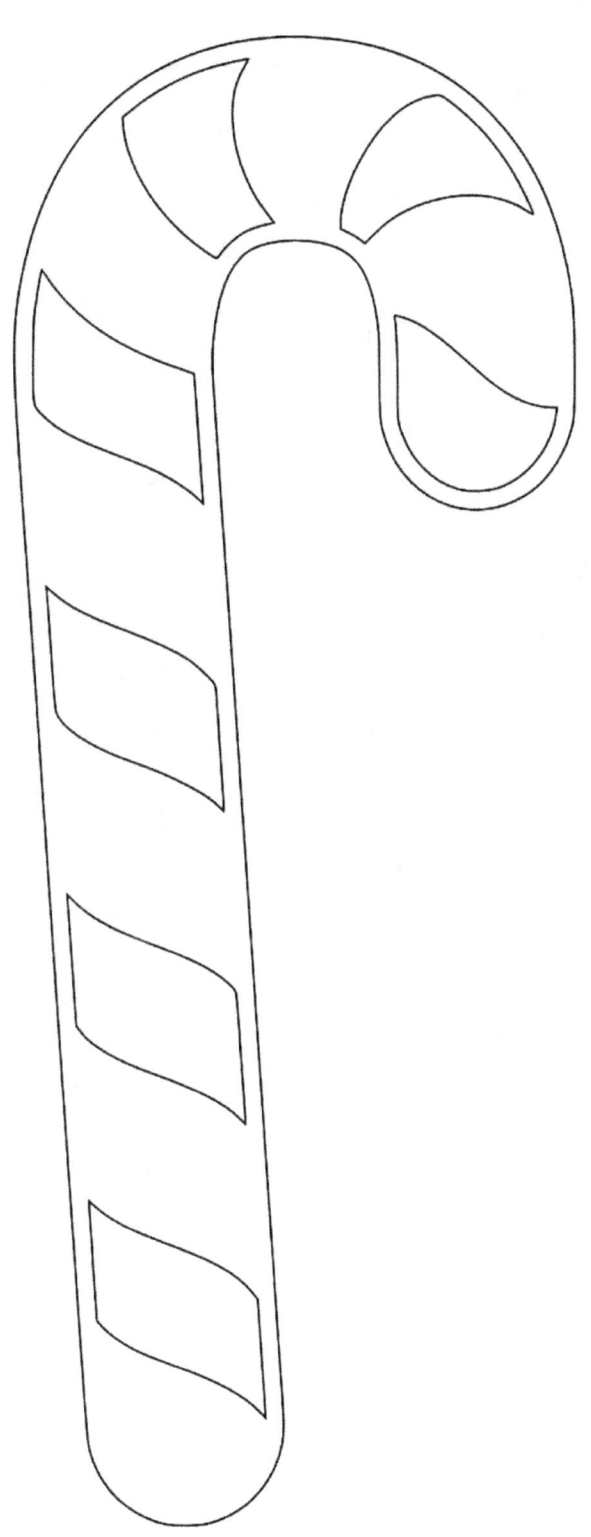

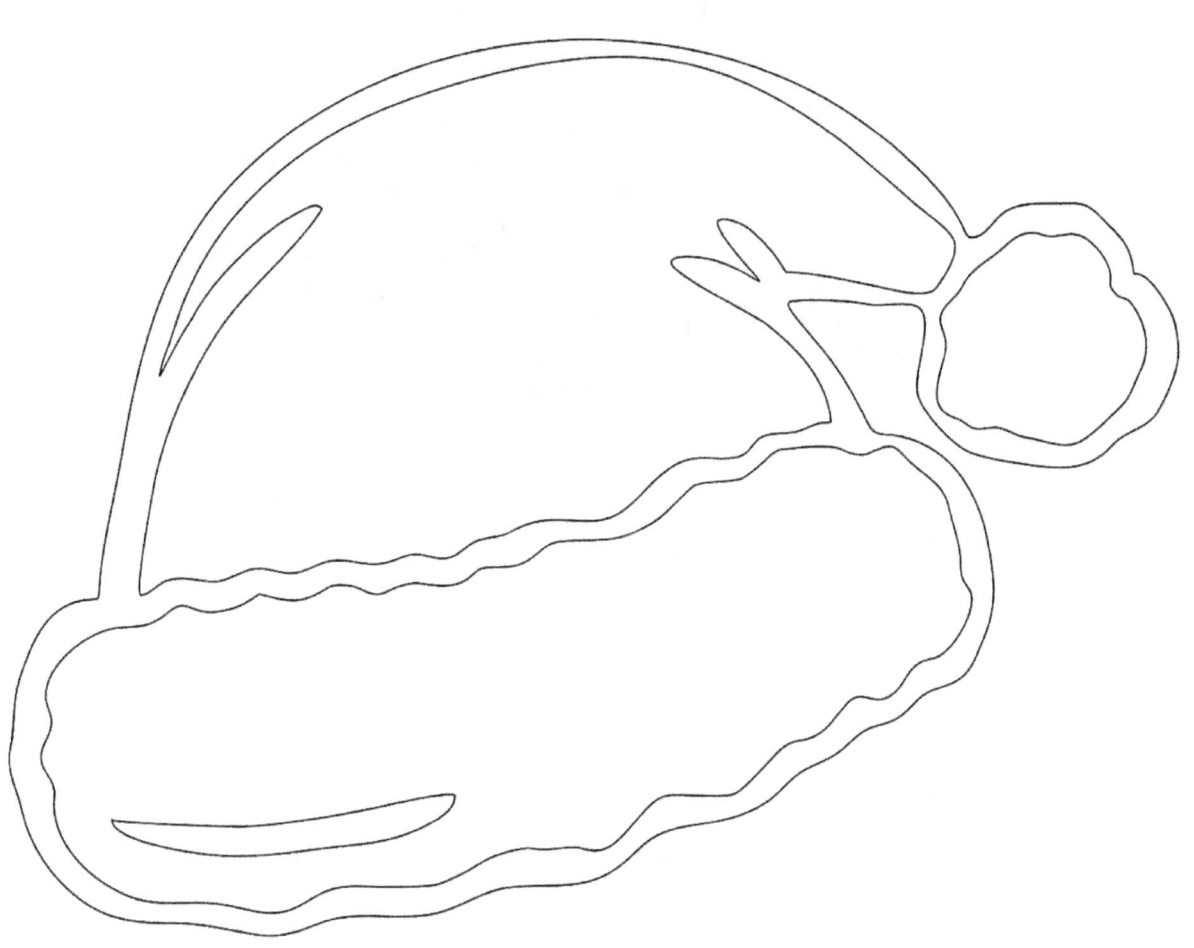